# COLORAD
## *San Juan Mountains*

### Text & Photography by Grant Collier

With Historic Images by Joseph Collier

## Collier Publishing
Lakewood, CO

©2008 Grant Collier
http://www.collierpublishing.com

ISBN #978-0-9769218-5-1

Design by Grant Collier and Elizabeth Greco
Printed in China

Above Photo: View of Mount Sneffels from the Dallas Divide during the height of fall color.
Title Page: Rugged mountain peaks rise above multicolored aspen along Owl Creek Pass.
Cover: Indian paintbrush thrive in Porphyry Basin at an elevation of nearly 13,000 feet.
Back Cover: Expansive view of the San Juan Mountains from a spot high above Stony Pass.
Author photo taken by Jose' Low.

Many thanks to Catamount Mayhugh and Dax Oliver, who gave me feedback on the text.

References:
Chronic, Halka & Williams, Felicie. *Roadside Geology of Colorado*. Missoula, Montana: Mountain Press Publishing Company, 2002.
Hopkins, Ralph & Lindy. *Hiking Colorado's Geology*. Seattle, WA: The Mountaineers, 2000.
Foutz, Dell. *Geology of Colorado Illustrated*. Grand Junction, CO: Your Geologist, 1994.

# About the Author

Grant Collier is a lifelong resident of Colorado. He grew up in the foothills above Denver and spent much of his childhood exploring Colorado's Rocky Mountains. Grant first took up photography while attending college in Los Angeles. He found endless photographic opportunities throughout the Desert Southwest while driving to and from L.A. After graduating from college in 1996, Grant began a photographic career that had him following, quite literally, in the footsteps of his great-great-grandfather, the pioneer photographer Joseph Collier. Grant traveled throughout Colorado taking photos from the exact same spots that Joseph had taken his images over one-hundred years earlier. These photographs were published in the book *Colorado: Yesterday & Today*, which was released in 2001. Since this time, Grant has continued exploring the Colorado wilderness, taking color photographs of his own design. These images have been published in the books *Colorado: Moments in Time, Colorado's Hidden Wonders, Colorado Wild*, and in a yearly Colorado wall calendar. Collier's work has also appeared in magazines across the United States and Europe and in art galleries throughout Colorado. Grant has several other Colorado photography books in the works and will also be publishing books on the Colorado Plateau and the American West. More information on Grant's photography can be found online at: gcollier.com and collierpublishing.com.

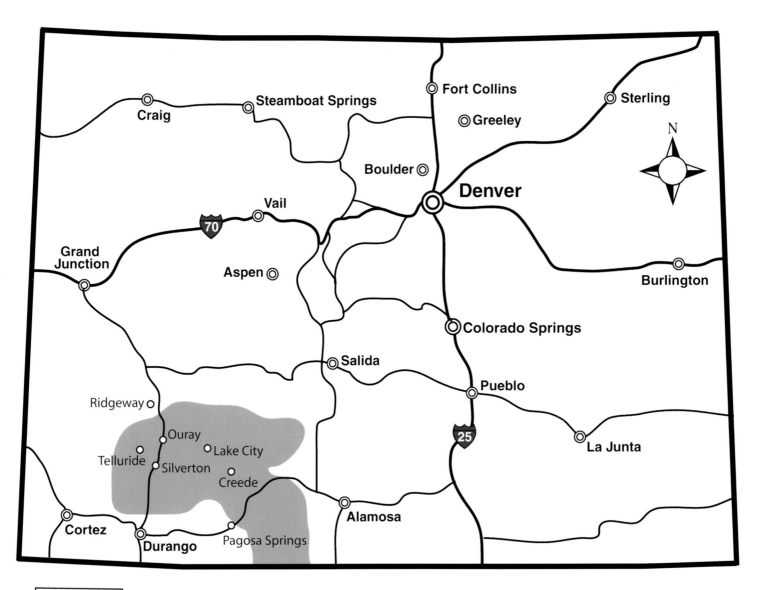

Craig · Steamboat Springs · Fort Collins · Sterling · Greeley · Boulder · Denver · N

Vail · 70 · Grand Junction · Aspen · Burlington · Colorado Springs · Salida · Pueblo · Ridgeway · Ouray · Lake City · Telluride · Silverton · Creede · 25 · La Junta · Cortez · Durango · Pagosa Springs · Alamosa

San Juan Mountains

# Foreword

The San Juan Mountains are one of those rare and magical places to which I am inexorably drawn. Although I grew up in Colorado and spent many days exploring its mountains, I did not venture to the San Juan Mountains until I was twenty-one years old. Since then, I have returned to the San Juans every year, photographing them through all of the changing seasons. Each time I return, I discover something new. This isn't because the San Juans are slow to reveal their secrets. Rather, the mountains are so vast and harbor such majestic scenery that one could never fully appreciate them, even after a lifetime of exploration.

For me, part of the appeal of the San Juan Mountains is the opportunity for dramatic photographs on both vast and intimate scales. When I first traveled to the San Juans, I was immediately struck by the enormous, glacially carved peaks rising skyward. But when I delved into the heart of the San Juans, I was amazed by the beauty and variety of smaller details that make up the landscape. There are lily pads floating in high alpine ponds, intricate whorls of bark on the sides of trees, and multicolored lichen covering imposing rock faces. And for brief periods of time each year, the mountains are filled first with an unimaginable number of wildflowers and then with endless expanses of yellow aspen leaves.

Perhaps the greatest thing about the San Juan Mountains is the absolute solitude that can be found there. The San Juans encompass seven different wilderness areas, containing nearly one million acres of primordial land. One could spend weeks wandering in the mountains without seeing another soul.

When I first ventured into a wilderness area in the San Juans, I was nearly overwhelmed by the utter silence around me. But when my ears adjusted to the absence of the cacophonous noises of modern society, I found that it really isn't so silent in the San Juans. There is the gentle rustling of grass as it waves in the mountain breeze, the muted roar of a far-off waterfall, and the melodious notes of an unseen bird. These sounds resonate with a primal spirit within us that knows we were born of this land and that we can always return to it to find solitude and peace of mind.

Grant Collier
Lakewood, Colorado

# Introduction

The story of the San Juan Mountains is a story of artistry executed on a grand scale by the forces of earth, fire, water, and ice. These forces have gradually transformed the region from a flat landscape near sea level into the enormous mountains that exist today. This transformation has occurred over such a vast length of time that the changes are almost imperceptible during a human lifetime.

The first stage of mountain-building in the San Juan region began approximately 70 million years ago, when the North American and Pacific continental plates collided. Weak parts of land on the Northern American plate were pushed upwards, forming the Rocky Mountains, which stretch from New Mexico to Alaska. In southwestern Colorado, this uplift resulted in a relatively modest formation known as the San Juan Dome.

Although the initial uplift was caused by plate tectonics, the San Juan Mountains were molded primarily by volcanic activity. From 36 to 30 million years ago, massive volcanoes churned out large amounts of magma, which covered much of the San Juan Dome. Over the following four million years, at least fifteen of the volcanoes erupted with cataclysmic force, spewing huge amounts of ash and rock across the land and causing the volcanoes to collapse into calderas as large as fifty miles across.

Mineralized fluids containing gold, silver, and other metals filled the faults created by these eruptions. Over 20 million years later, these mineral deposits would give rise to the gold and silver rush to the San Juan Mountains in the late 19th century.

The violent volcanic eruptions were followed by more moderate volcanic activity beginning approximately 26 million years ago. This activity finally began to subside around 22 million years ago, leaving behind a massive volcanic plateau. Approximately 10 million years ago, large streams began to erode this plateau and carve distinctive peaks and valleys throughout the landscape.

Evidence of volcanic activity can be found in every part of the San Juan Mountains. One such place is Wheeler Geologic Area, located near the town of Creede. This region was covered with large amounts of volcanic ash following an eruption from the San Luis caldera approximately 26 million years ago. Most of the ash has long since eroded away, but a portion of it can still be seen today in this fascinating geologic wonderland.

Another dramatic volcanic remnant is Lizard Head Peak, located southwest of the town of Telluride. This tall, narrow formation is a volcanic neck, which was created when lava solidified inside the vent of an active volcano. The surrounding rock later eroded away, exposing the neck. Geologists speculate that 14,000-foot Mount Sneffels may also be the neck of an immense volcano.

Although the San Juan Mountains were created by fire, they were sculpted by ice. Beginning approximately 1.8 million years ago, a series of ice ages engulfed the planet. Massive glaciers formed throughout the San Juan Mountains. As the glaciers gradually moved down the mountainsides, they carved the deep valleys and jagged peaks that are characteristic of the region today.

Signs of glacial activity can be seen throughout the mountain range. One of the largest glaciers was located between Red Mountain Pass and the town of Ridgeway, where it carved out an impressive canyon and valley. The area around Lake San Cristobal, near Lake City, was also exposed to intense glacial activity.

When the glaciers last receded around 10,000 years ago, many life forms that were unable to survive in the harsher conditions were able to recolonize the area. Due to the wide range of elevations and the multitude of different climates, nine distinct ecosystems have formed in the San Juan Mountains. Wildlife populations in the area include mule deer, elk, black bear, bighorn sheep, and the lynx, which was reintroduced to the region in 1999. The mountains are also the last known location for certain arctic mosses that are relics of the last ice age.

The first Native Americans arrived in Colorado approximately 12,000 years ago, but no tribes are known to have established settlements in the San Juans until the Ute Indians arrived around 1300 A.D. Unlike their predecessors who relied on farming in lower elevations, the Utes were a nomadic people who subsisted as hunters and gatherers. In 1873, the Utes were displaced from the San Juan Mountains by American prospectors who came in search of silver and gold.

In the years following the arrival of the white settlers, large tracts of land have been transformed by mining and development. However, with the creation of seven wilderness areas, much of the land remains as remote and primal as it was when colossal volcanoes were spewing lava across the landscape or when tremendous glaciers were slowly, but persistently scouring the mountains.

*Left:* 14,000-foot Mount Sneffels is reflected in a small pond along the Dallas Divide.

*Right:* A small puddle that formed after heavy rains reflects barren aspen trees in late autumn.

*Left: Lily pads float in a small pond along Molas Pass above Silverton.*

*Right: Sunflowers populate an alpine meadow below Stony Mountain near Yankee Boy Basin.*

*Waterfalls tumble down steep mountain slopes below the Golden Horn and Ice Lake Basin.*

*A solitary cloud floats above a forest of pine trees located along South Fork Creek.*

*Columbines grow in abundance throughout American Basin, near Lake City.*

*The Mountain Top Mine has withstood the ravages of time in Governor Basin.*

*Wildflowers grow below Sheep Mountain near the summit of Stony Pass.*

*Pink and yellow paintbrush thrive below Stony Mountain near Governor Basin.*

*Left: A jagged aspen-bole fence is illuminated by early morning light along West Dallas Road.*

*Right: The head frame of the Yankee Girl Mine, which was built in the early 1880s, remains standing on the slopes of Red Mountain #2.*

*Left: 13,000-foot Lizard Head Peak in the western San Juan Mountains is a remnant of an ancient volcano.*

*Right: A patchwork of pine trees and aspen trees dots a hillside in the San Juan National Forest.*

*The last light of the day illuminates peaks of the Grenadier Range, which are reflected in Molas Lake.*

*Low-lying clouds hover over Molas Lake on a rainy day in July.*

*A jagged peak rises above a vast expanse of rolling hills known as the Highlands in the Weminuche Wilderness.*

*Last Dollar Road winds its way between a grove of aspen trees during the height of fall color.*

*Peaks of the Sneffels Range rise above vast expanses of aspen and pine trees along the Dallas Divide.*

*Numerous icicles hang from a rock face near the town of Rico.*

*North Clear Creek Falls plunges 100 feet over a cliff face near Lake City.*

*Dramatic clouds are reflected in a small lily pond along Molas Pass.*

*Left: Aspen and pine trees are reflected in Crystal Lake along Red Mountain Pass.*

*Right: A high alpine pond near Clear Lake reflects the mountain scenery at dusk.*

*Dramatic clouds hover over imposing rock formations along Owl Creek Pass.*

*A small natural arch sits high atop a hillside above the Dolores River.*

*Left: A small, picturesque waterfall flows along Sneffels Creek in Yankee Boy Basin.*

*Right: A larger waterfall plunges over jagged rocks in Yankee Boy Basin.*

# San Juans' Past

*A Collection of Historic Images by
Pioneer Photographer Joseph Collier*

When the San Juan Mountains were first settled by American pioneers, photography was a very new craft. Only a few intrepid men hauled their heavy camera equipment to these remote mountains to record the early mining days on glass plate negatives. One such man was Joseph Collier.

Joseph Collier was born in Aberdeenshire, Scotland in 1836. He worked as a blacksmith until a debilitating back injury forced him to quit his job in the early 1860s. While recuperating, he learned the new art of photography and soon turned this into a career. Joseph photographed many influential citizens, including the Prince of Wales, who later became King Edward VII. He was also one of the first photographers to experiment with photographic enlargements. The *British Journal of Photography* wrote that "in the mammoth productions of Mr. Collier we find the highest excellence that we have yet seen."

Despite Joseph's considerable achievements in Scotland, he decided to move with his wife and four children to Central City, Colorado in 1871. He set up a photography studio and began photographing the mountains, mining towns, and early residents. Many of these photographs were sold as postcards in the eastern United States.

While in Central City, Collier continued to push the boundaries of photographic technology. In 1872, he acquired one of the world's fastest photographic lenses, and in 1874 he became the first photographer west of the Mississippi to print positive images onto glass.

Joseph Collier made his first visit to the San Juan Mountains in 1883. He photographed most of the burgeoning mining towns, along with the breathtaking scenery. This visit came during the height of mining activity in the San Juan Mountains. The mines were producing large amounts of silver and gold, and the streets in the nearby towns were bustling with activity.

Only ten years before, white settlers were unfamiliar with this region, as it was inhabited by the Ute Indians. The Utes, who called the land the "Shining Mountains," had lived in relative peace in the area for over five-hundred years. In 1873, however, they were pressured into signing the Brunot

Agreement, which reduced the size of their reservation and opened the San Juans for mining. Shortly afterwards, a large rush of prospectors descended on the land and established mining camps throughout the mountains.

Although much gold and silver was discovered, the early days were tough, as there were few roads and no railroads with which to transport supplies. This problem was alleviated by Otto Mears, who constructed three narrow gauge railroads and over four hundred miles of toll roads in the San Juans.

As transportation improved, the mining towns began to flourish. Many banks, hotels, churches, and saloons were constructed throughout the region in the early 1880s. This prosperity came to an abrupt end in 1893 when Congress repealed the Sherman Act, which had guaranteed the purchase of silver by the federal government. Silver prices plummeted and many of the mines in the area were forced to close.

The economy recovered in the late 1890s when large amounts of gold were discovered near Telluride, Silverton, and Lake City. This recovery was tarnished by two long and bitter strikes by mine workers in Telluride in 1901 and 1903. These strikes resulted in much violence, and the National Guard had to be called in to restore order.

Following the strikes, mining began to decline and many of the residents moved away. Those who remained were hit by a terrible flu epidemic that swept through Colorado in 1919. This epidemic ravaged the town of Silverton, killing over ten percent of its inhabitants.

Following this tragedy, only the largest mines in the area, including the great Sunnyside Mine, continued to operate. However, during World War II all non-essential mining was banned by the federal government and the remaining gold and silver mines were shut down.

Today, tourism has replaced mining as the primary industry in the San Juans. However, residents still proudly hang onto their past. Numerous buildings from the 1800s remain in use and old mining structures dot the landscape. These structures provide lasting testament to a brief but extraordinary period in Colorado's San Juan Mountains.

View of Telluride in the 1880s depicts bustling activity on the town's main street.

View of Silverton in 1883 shows many buildings that have survived to the present day.

In the 1880s, Lake City was a prosperous but wild mining town.

364 LAKE HOUSE, LAKE SAN MIGUEL

Early pioneers stand in front of a lake house on Lake San Miguel, now known as Trout Lake.

343 ON BURRO PARK ROAD

View from near the summit of Burro Park Road, now called Cinnamon Pass.

Mystic Falls has remained largely unchanged
since this image was taken in the 1880s.

A passenger train of the D&RG railroad
stops along its route near Silverton.

TOLL ROAD ABOVE OPHIR

View of the toll road along Ophir Pass, located near the town of Telluride.

The North Star Mine near Silverton produced large amounts of gold and silver.

A team of donkeys stands outside the Dyer Mine near Silverton. Pack trains such as this one were the primary means of transporting supplies to and from the mines.

A team of pack donkeys stand in a street in the town of Ames, located near Telluride.

Red Mountain Town was devastated by fire twice in its short but eventful history.

The long-abandoned town of Congress was located on the south side of Red Mountain Pass.

The town of Eureka was built near the site of the first gold discovery in the San Juan Mountains.

At an elevation of 11,600 feet, Animas Forks was a great place for mining but a tough place to live.

Summitville was a prosperous mining town in the 1880s. In the 1990s, it became a Superfund site.

*Left: Bridal Veil Falls rises above moss-covered boulders near the town of Telluride.*

*Right: Rose paintbrush grows near Governor Basin in the Uncompahgre National Forest.*

*An old wooden fence winds its way along the Dallas Divide near Ridgeway.*

*Dew drops cover a cluster of fallen aspen leaves in the Uncompahgre Wilderness.*

*Left: A mountain stream flows through a field of wildflowers below Clear Lake.*

*Right: View of Red Mountain #1 from the slopes of Brown Mountain.*

*Left: Numerous aspen trees are reflected in Rowdy Lake near Owl Creek Pass.*

*Right: Close up shot of natural grass and aspen leaves in Rowdy Lake.*

*Wilson Peak and Gladstone Peak rise above a snow-covered field near Telluride.*

*Long evening shadows loom over a small pine tree on a steep mountain slope.*

*Massive icicles hang on the walls of Box Canyon in early winter in Ouray.*

*View of pine trees in a snow-covered meadow along Lizard Head Pass.*

*Left: Low-lying clouds are reflected in Little Molas Lake along Molas Pass.*

*Right: Bundles of hay are lined up in a breathtaking ranch below 14,000-foot Mount Sneffels.*

*Left: Conejos Falls plunges over a cliff face in the South San Juan Wilderness.*

*Right: Impressive rock formations rise above aspen and pine trees along Owl Creek Pass.*

*Red Mountain #1 is reflected in a small pond in Gray Copper Gulch.*

*Jagged volcanic rocks rise above an old forest in Wheeler Geologic Area, near the town of Creede.*

*Left: Close up view of aspen trees in the Uncompahgre National Forest.*

*Right: Indian Paintbrush thrive below an impressive waterfall in Porphyry Basin.*

*Far Right: A waterfall along Red Mountain Pass begins its descent down steep mountain terrain.*

*Bizarre, crooked aspen trees populate part of a forest along Owl Creek Pass.*

*Left: View from the south side of Imogene Pass following a severe hail storm.*

*Right: A lone, deceased tree stands along a cliff face near Yankee Boy Basin.*

*A layer of snow covers a forest of pine trees along Wolf Creek Pass.*

*Snow from an early winter storm enshrouds trees in the Rio Grande National Forest.*

*Left:* Two small, intertwined aspen trees rise above a carpet of aspen leaves on Miller Mesa.

*Right:* Mystic Falls drops into a deep canyon near the western edge of the San Juan Mountains.

*A rainbow emerges above mountains in the Silverton Group as the sun sets to the west.*

*A solitary spruce tree grows amidst a large stand of aspen in late fall.*

*A small stream flows through rugged mountain terrain in the La Plata Mountains.*